MATTHEW ESPINOSA

MORE THAN ME

Photos on pages i, ii, iv, v, vi–vii, x–xi, 1, 3, 17, 20, 21, 33, 34–35, 38, 39, 40–41, 42–43, 44, 45, 46, 47, 50–51, 52, 55, 56, 58–59, 61, 62, 64, 65, 66, 70–71, 72, 74–75, 76–77, 78–79, 80, 82–83, 84–85, 86, 92, 97, 98, 108, 110–1, 112–3, 116–7, 118, 120–1, 123, 124, 125, 128–9, 131, 138, 139, 146–7, 148, 149, 150–1, 152–3, 154–5, 157, 160–1, 162, 165, 166, 168–9, 170, 171, 181, 186–7, 188, 191, 192, 195, 198–9, 200, 202, 203, 204, 206, 210, 211, and 212 courtesy of Chris Eckert.

Photos on pages 6–7, 10–11, 13, 14–15, 18, 19, 22, 23, 26–27, 28, 30–31, 36–37, 90–91, 94–95, 96–97, 98–99, 100, 101, 103, 104–5, 106–7, 134–5, 136, 140–1, and 142–3 courtesy of the author.

Photo on page 63 and drawings on pages 187–189, 191, 192, and 195 by Works Well With Others, LLC.

Photos on pages 54, 63, 142–3, 163, 164, 167, and 207 courtesy of Shutterstock.

Photos on pages 174–5, 176, 178, and 182 © Digital Echo, LLC. All rights reserved. Used with permission.

Photo on page 208 by Jesse Grant / WireImage / Getty Images.

HarperCollins

Matthew Espinosa: More Than Me
Copyright © 2017 by Matthew Lee, LLC
All rights reserved. Manufactured in China. No part of this book may be used or reproduced in any manner whatsoever without written permission except in the case of brief quotations embodied in critical articles and reviews. For information address HarperCollins Children's Books, a division of HarperCollins Publishers, 195 Broadway, New York, NY 10007.
www.epicreads.com
ISBN 978-0-06-249080-3
Typography by Works Well With Others, LLC
Art direction by Alison Klapthor

16 17 18 19 20   SCP   10 9 8 7 6 5 4 3 2 1
❖
First Edition

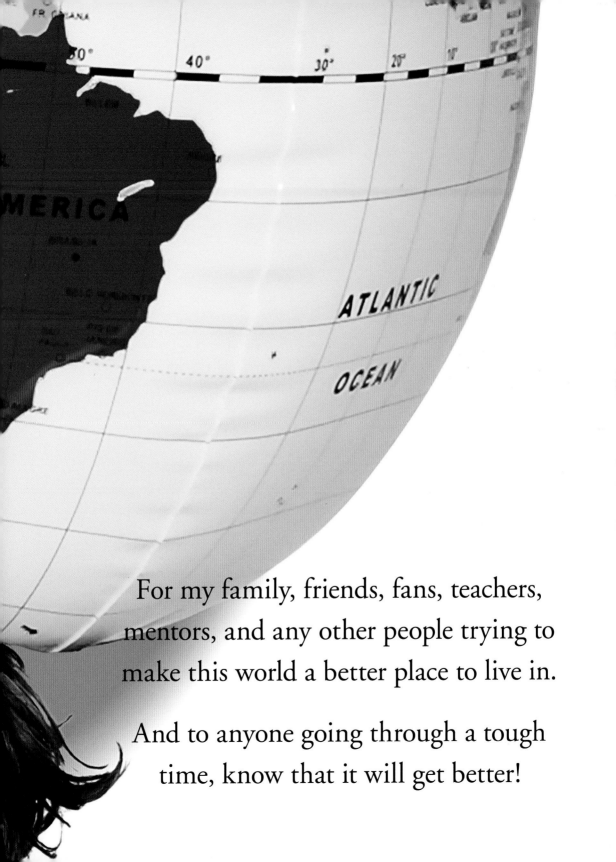

For my family, friends, fans, teachers, mentors, and any other people trying to make this world a better place to live in.

And to anyone going through a tough time, know that it will get better!

“ **I want to be communicator, someone who to my peers**

**a motivator, a
a influencer;
projects positivity
and the world. "**

HEY!

It's Matthew!

I've got a lot to share—much more than I could ever put in a six-second Vine, an Instagram caption, a quick YouTube video, or a tweet of 140 characters or less. And none of the above tells you much about who I *really* am as a person. What you've gotten up till now was just scratching the surface. So, faced with the question "What's the best way to give my fans a real, deep, intimate picture of myself?" a book seemed like a good choice. I mean, that's a lot of pages to fill up, and they can always make the type *really* small if I go on and on. My teachers didn't call me chatty for nothin'. . . .

1

Truth is, there's a broad spectrum of who I am, who I'm not, what gets me going as a human being, what I like, what I don't like, and what makes this a joyful life to live. I have visions, goals, and dreams, and I've done a lot of growing up over the past few years. It's kind of crazy when I think about it: how far I've come in such a short amount of time. How? Why? I couldn't tell you 100 percent. I'm blessed, that's for sure. Looking over my life in this way helps me appreciate it even more. I get to take a step back and really be grateful to the people who got me here. Without God, my family, friends, teachers, coaches, mentors, and fans, I'd be nowhere—so shout-out to y'all. Thanks to you, I'm in LA, following my passion and my purpose, with an incredible support group behind me.

And I want to put that back out there to everyone flipping these pages: I believe in you, too, and I know that we can be legendary together. I love it when someone tells me, "Hey, you gave me confidence. You taught me to be myself." If there's one thing I hope you take away from my story, it's this: every person has a voice and every life has a purpose. Personally, I want to be a motivator, a communicator, an influencer, someone who projects positivity to my peers and the world. I will keep working for you—your love and support don't go unnoticed!—because I believe it's my purpose and duty to do so. And if I make you smile or laugh in the process, that's even cooler. And if that isn't enough, there's all these totally embarrassing personal pictures of me that I let my mom dig up.

Enjoy and love you,

Matthew Espinosa

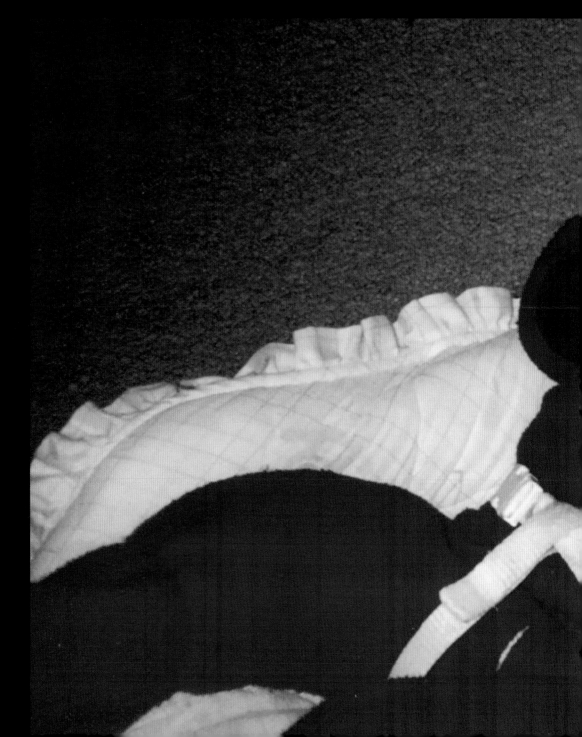

LET'S START AT THE BEGINNING

When I came along, my sister, Kristen, was nine, and my brothers, Ryan and Dylan, were seven and two. Yup, I'm the baby of the family, and they never let me forget it. My parents will tell you that, from day one, I was one happy little dude. Somewhat adventurous, sure, but never jumping off the walls or acting crazy like a lot of other boys. My mom insists I didn't give her a hard time and thanks me for it. If she put me in a time-out, I'd just go stand in the corner by the stairwell. Dylan would try to argue his way out of it, but I knew better. I knew

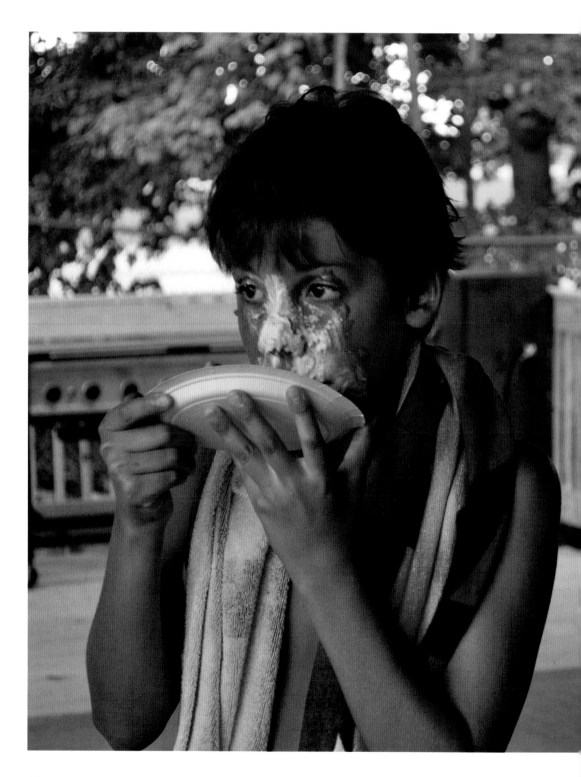

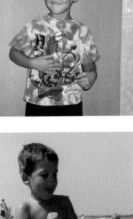

by the time he was done arguing and just beginning his time-out, I'd be out of mine and already back outside playing. You did the crime, do the time!

I have a summer birthday, so I started kindergarten at St. Thomas Aquinas Regional School a little late. I was six and the class clown who cracked the other kids up. When my mom would ask the teachers at parent/teacher conferences, "How's Matthew doing?" they'd all say, "Oh, he's doing great . . . but he's a little bit chatty." Couldn't help it; I always had something to say (and still do).

I was into sports, big time. From the time I was four, I did soccer in the spring and fall. When I was in first grade, around seven years old, I started swim team, and that went on until high school. I also did T-ball, basketball, and lacrosse. I wanted to play football, but my mom wouldn't let me start until I was ten—that was her magic number. As much as I begged and tried to wear her down, she said no. So I played other sports and waited for the day I turned double digits and, when I did, Mom caved. All in all, I'd have to say football and lacrosse were definitely my favorites, although each sport and team really has a special place in my memories.

Despite all the sporty stuff, I guess it was pretty clear from the start that I would grow up to do something creative. I believe I got all my comedic personality and the ability to speak so well from my dad. I loved to make my family laugh, pretending to be different characters. My fave was this little old man with a cane. I'd play him hitting on my mom and sister. My whole family would be in tears cracking up. Jim Carrey was my favorite actor on the planet, and I wanted to grow up and *be* him. Starting in fourth grade, whenever we were given a group

project in school, other kids would want to do a diorama, a poster, or a book report. Me? I would always be the one to say, "Can we do a video?" I also did a lot of stuff with photos—I loved to make montages with music. I remember starting in fourth grade doing lip-synching videos with Dylan. In middle school, I did acting and theater, and honestly, that's where I want to be headed one day. I'd think about being a serious actor, someone like Leonardo DiCaprio, with a wide range of roles that challenge me.

From the time my parents bought me a mini video camera of my own, I never put it down. It was really apparent to everyone who knew me that I was into tech and videos, editing and filmmaking. But remember, this was before social media became really popular. So I had all these crazy ideas exploding in my head, and no way to set them loose into the world. Once I discovered YouTube, I started making videos and posting them all the time. I remember every weekend I'd go over to my friend Johnny's house and we'd shoot. The best part for me was editing the videos on Movie Maker: putting them together so they told a story, adding music and sound effects. Gradually, I started learning newer, harder editing programs to really bring them to life. In fourth grade, while most kids would be on their computers playing basic games, I'd be there at my screen at home, splicing videos on Sony Vegas Pro 10.

The rest, as they say, is history. But really, it was more than that. It was destiny, fate, whatever you wanna call it. Something just clicked for me and I knew this was gonna be my thing—the thing that set me apart, the thing that let me reach out to others in a powerful way. But that said, I never labeled myself or let people label me. I had tons of interests and things I liked to do. I never wanted to be just part of one group, and I would try and break down walls of cliques and bring people from all walks of life together. I believe you should be friends with everyone because everyone has something significant to bring to the table. That's who I was, and I'm proud to say it's who I am today. It's our differences that make us who we are—so why would you wanna mess with that?

Despite all the sporty stuff, I guess it was pretty clear from the start that I would grow up to do something creative.

#**ASK**MATT

What was your fave subject in elementary school?

Probably PE. I know it sounds like a cliché, but I liked anything physical and active. I liked it so much more than just sitting behind a desk. Gotta keep movin'. Even today, my body is always in motion. I can't sit still! My feet are actually tapping while I'm writing this. . . .

Did you ever get detention?

Even though I was the class clown and pretty rambunctious, I somehow always managed to stay out of detention. I could talk myself out of anything, that's for sure. I think my whole life I only got one detention—and

that was for hugging a teacher. I know, bizarre. It was sophomore year in high school and I was talking out of turn and my teacher got mad at me. So I got up out of my seat, apologized, and tried to hug it out with her as a joke. Well, she didn't think it was funny. She freaked and sent me to detention. Lesson learned—not everyone gets my

sense of humor or likes warm hugs. . . .

What would you tell your younger self if you could?

I'd say, "Matthew! Dude! Check out these apps! Your whole world will change, man, if you get on them now. Start Vining! Get a handle on your Twitter handle!" But wait . . . mini Matthew doesn't have a phone. Scratch that.

Ten things nobody knows about me

(But now you do 'cause I just spilled . . .)

01 I was obsessed with computers back in the day. You had to pry my fingers off the keyboard. . . .

02 I was an Xbox maniac back in the day. Halo 2, anyone?

03 I try and eat healthy *most* of the time, but I do love pretty much any kind of cereal—straight out of the box. I've never met a flake, an O, or a Krispie I didn't like.

04 I've been playing sports since I was four years old. Or probably since I was in diapers. I've always been someone who needs to get his energy out in a very physical way.

05 Big beds used to scare me. I'd always imagine some creepy clown or slasher/ax murderer hiding underneath or maybe I'd roll over and they'd be there next to me. I've mostly gotten over it, but every now and then it's still a little eerie. . . .

06 I want to learn to wakeboard. Never done it. Need to do it.

07 I hate soda. All I drink is milk, water, and orange juice. Must be something about the bubbles.

08 When I was on the swim team, I wore speedos instead of jammers and it was dope. I'm sorry—all the best swimmers on the team would wear them, so I had to catch up. And no, I'm not showing you a pic. Use your imagination.

09 I want to skydive—but only after I've accomplished more things of significance in my life. Ya know, just in case the chute doesn't open. . . .

10 I want to learn how to cook. My mom will tell you it's because I can't boil water. But I'm a good eater, so cooking just seems a wise skill to have, don't you think?

#**ASK**MATT

Did you ever go to prom?

I did! I decided it was something everyone should experience in life. So I rearranged my crazy travel schedule, hopped a plane from Dubai, and went to my senior prom back in Virginia. I hadn't really been back in my Bishop Ireton High School community for a year, so it felt a little awkward and weird at first. But overall, it was a great night and I'm glad I didn't miss it. And I did almost miss it—if one of our flights had been delayed, it would have messed everything up. But I made it in time (extremely jet-lagged), put on a tux, and went with my friend Drake. The music was great and I pretty much danced with my guy friends all night (there was kind of a mosh-pit thing goin' on). Everyone acted fairly normal, although the principal did ask to take a selfie with me. I felt really blessed that I could do this, that I could go home to my high school and experience prom and then go back to my life in LA. I thought maybe I'd feel sad or I'd regret missing my junior and senior year, but I didn't feel that at all. If anything, it just affirmed for me that the choice I made— leaving Virginia and going to LA—was the right one. I'm following my dreams. But it's nice to know you can always go home and the people who care about you don't stop caring.

AMOUS

ME AND THE INTERNET

I was bored one day and downloaded the Vine app—truly, that's how it all began. Me yawning and twiddling my thumbs, going, "So what can I do that I haven't done before?" I started making Vines and one of them went big and, well, you know the rest of the story. It really made sense and felt like the next step for me: I already liked making people laugh, so this was a way to take it broader, to reach a bigger audience, to get my voice out there. Did I ever think for a second I would hit seven figures on followers? No way. When I got a million followers it was surreal—and I feel like Twitter and Instagram all stemmed from the fans from Vine. It was a great feeling, a huge accomplishment: a million people liked me enough to click a button and follow me. It made me keep

Lots of amazing experiences throughout the years, like Creative Collab Tour; interviews with cool people; having my family at events, including my half sister, Melanie; and hanging with Larry King

going and putting content out there. It led to the MAGCON Tour, where I toured with people who soon came to be some of my closest friends and still are to this day. It also led to other tours, meet-and-greets, events, and interviews.

I was a reluctant Viner in the beginning. I didn't even want to download the app, and a friend convinced me. I was like, "Fine, fine, fine, I'll do it—stop nagging." My very first one was me on the couch hangin' with my friend. Just silly stuff. From there on, I just got more creative, and then one went viral. It was me listening to a Marvin Gaye song. My shirt was on in the beginning, but then I'm listening to the song and off it comes—because that's what Marvin Gaye music does to you.

People ask me all the time, "How did you do it?" Honestly, I was honest. I was myself. I was 100 percent Matthew Espinosa. What you see is me: how my mind works, all the crazy, creative, out-of-the-box things that go through my head on a daily basis. Maybe you were thinking the same thing I was, but I'm the guy who will say it, loud and proud. What's in my head is out of my mouth a second later. Like, you're watching all these kids graduating high school and throwing their caps up in the air and you wanna shout, "Hey, why are you doing that? You're just gonna have to pick them up later." Or you see a group of girls all get up and go to the bathroom together at dinner and think, "Hey, what would happen if guys did that? How funny would that look?" A lot of my Vines and videos start with that concept of "what if?" I'm a pretty curious guy—I want to know how and why things happen. Will I ever run out of material? Nah. Because life in

I was a reluctant Viner in the beginning. I didn't even want to download the app.

general is unpredictable and nonsensical (is that a real word? It kind of sounds like a Dr. Seuss one). I think people laugh when something makes them see themselves or their situation in a new light. So I spend a lot of my time considering "the little things," "the small stuff" that we all sweat. I try to bring a fresh perspective to it, to make you think about it differently. I guess you could say I look at life with a question mark: What's really

going on here? Is that super-annoying situation a chance to laugh out loud? I think it is. It kind of defuses the annoyingness—POOF! Be gone with you!

With Vines, I had to learn how to piece my ideas together into a really quick, impactful video. Six seconds goes by in a blink (although, if you Google it, most people blink every four seconds—just sayin'). It does challenge me. Creative is one thing, but quick and creative is a whole different ball game. When I'm coming up with content, I have to literally envision telling a story in a blip. In the beginning, some of my Vines were just silly for the sake of being silly—kind of immature, middle school practical-joke stuff (burping, farting, making funny faces). But now, I realize the best Vines not only make you laugh, they make you think.

How to become a social media star
(in five easy steps)

01

Be yourself.

Find the one thing you love doing and put it out there. I've seen musicians and actors get their start on Vine or YouTube by just sharing their passion. If you act like someone you're not (just to get followers), people see right through it. Be genuine.

02

Be realistic.

Don't assume it'll happen overnight. Your motivation should never be "I wanna be famous." It should be "I wanna share what I love doing most with other people." If the only thing driving you is fame, you might as well pack it up right now. Review step one.

03

Be a good communicator.

By this, I mean figure out what you want to say and the most effective way to put it across. Think about your words and the impact they have. Think about images that go with those words. What are you trying to say and what's your reason for saying it? A lot of kids just post or Vine for the sake of putting something out there. But I really actually put a lot of thought into those six seconds.

04 | 05

Know your audience.

Who are you talking to? Who are your followers? What do they want and expect from you? I could tell early on what kind of Vines appealed most (usually the funny stuff) and what my fans wanted to hear from me just from seeing what got the most likes and comments. You have to keep this in mind when you put stuff out there. You should be working hard to gain people's respect and trust.

Be consistent.

Keep the content coming. You can't be lazy if you want to be a social media star. You have to keep churning out quality content or your fans will lose interest. You've got their attention, so you need to work hard at keeping it. You have to continually be trying to up the bar.

On My Way to LA

I knew I'd wind up on the West Coast one day—my whole family did. My dad started calling me "Mr. Hollywood" when I was five. I did school plays all the time and loved it. In fifth grade, I was an orphan in the play *Oliver!*, in sixth grade a crapshooter in *Guys and Dolls*, in seventh grade a Hun in *Mulan*, and in eighth grade one of the brothers in *Seven Brides for Seven Brothers*. For a while, I thought I would become an actor on Broadway and live in New York City. But then, with my social media success, the timing seemed perfect to try my hand in Hollywood. It came on quicker than I ever imagined, and I'm really appreciative of that. My brother Ryan was graduating college, and we talked to my parents about letting us move out to LA together. I said I could do online schooling and prom-

I'm a family man, so it was hard to leave my mom and dad so early on in my life.

ised to keep up my grades (not an easy task when you're focusing on your career full-time). I said I would work hard and not goof off (too much) and Ryan would make sure I kept to my word. It took close to five months of conversations, but in the end, my parents knew there were too many opportunities happening to let them pass by and finally decided to let us go. How lucky am I to have a family that really supports me? 'Cause not all parents would be cool with it. But mine were. They trust me and believe in me and my dreams.

In the fall of 2014, my dad, Ryan, and I flew out to Los Angeles and started looking for a place to live. After a lot of searching, we finally decided on a place in Beverly Hills. My dad stayed with us for a couple months until we were settled, but then he went back to Virginia. Being on my own, even though I had Ryan with me, was a little scary at first, but I knew it was going to be a good experience. And thankfully, a few months later, my sister, Kristen, finished grad school and decided to live and work in LA, too. It's been so awesome to have two of my siblings with me through this journey, but of course I miss the rest of my family very much.

On that note, I have my regrets about it here and there: I'm a family man, so it was hard to leave my mom and dad so early on in my life. Also, since my brother Dylan is only two years older than me, we are very close. I always hung out with him and went to him with any questions, and he

was also really good with ideas for content. So it was difficult for me to be away from him. I visit Dylan at college as much as I can and, fortunately, I get to see my family either in California, Virginia, or while on tour every couple months. Besides that, we talk on the phone and text a lot! I miss my friends back home and my school, too. But I've learned to live with my decisions, and I know this is the right road. I'm glad I made the choices I made. You can't be an actor and make movies and still be a regular kid in school, playing sports and hanging with your friends. You have to make some sacrifices along the way. My friends are still my friends, and they understand and are proud of me. When I go back home, we pick up where we left off, as if nothing's happened.

I don't think I could ever go back. Don't get me wrong—I love to visit and my parents will never be able to get rid of the stuff in my room. But I feel like I'm on this path, this journey. No turning back till I get where I wanna be.

#**ASK**MATT

What has been your fave fan experience?
Probably stage diving at my first MAGCON event. I didn't look, I just leaped, and you guys were there to catch me. Love you! And thanks for preventing me from winding up in a full-body cast!

What's the one thing you want your fans to know about you?
That I'm someone who believes he—and you—can make a difference in the world. I want to be a force for change and I want my fans to do something, be something. Bring about the world we want to live in. We're a really powerful generation.

What's the weirdest thing you've been asked to autograph?
Body parts, probably. I've been asked to sign a few and I'm just not goin' there. . . .

FEW OF MY (NOT FAVORITE THINGS

SO)

(03)

THINGS I DON'T DIG...

We all have our pet peeves—you know, the little stuff that kind of gets under your skin and irritates you, like itchy underwear? Well, these are some of mine. Sometimes a guy's gotta vent. . . .

Burgers with not enough sauce

It can really ruin my culinary experience, you know? A dry burger is majorly disappointing. I always have to order extra sauce on the side just to be certain I'm not faced with a sauce-skimping situation after I've waited on that long, long line. . . .

Spicy food

It makes my mouth burn, my eyes water, my whole body heat up, and I have to ask myself, "Why?" Why interfere with the taste and enjoyment of your meal by firing it up? If I want my tongue and lips to be numb for three hours, I'll go to the dentist. I get that people like it—and you're entitled to your opinion and your three-alarm chili—but that's just not for me. Keep those hot peppers and Tabasco sauce far, far away.

Long lines

Especially when you're in a rush and you're starving. Fast food is supposed to be *fast* food, right? And it always happens when I have no time—I'm late to be somewhere and I have to grab a bite or I'm gonna pass out. My timing is flawless. When I need food fast, it's when everyone else on the planet decides they also need to order lunch. It's also a given that if there are eight lines to choose from, I will choose the slowest. It will look like it's short, but there's a reason: it knows I'm coming.

Popcorn kernels

They get stuck in your teeth and you can't pick them out, not even with a toothpick or dental floss. You need a tow truck to pry those kernels loose.

Being sick/injured

Sucks. Big time. It used to bug me a lot when I was on sports teams in high school and I was sick or injured and laid up in bed. So not only did I feel awful, but I felt guilty for not being there to help out my team. Being sick puts your entire life on hold, and I think that's

what irritates me the most. I hate to be in limbo. I hate when stuff is out of my control and I can't fix the situation. I hate to wait. Any ailment can do it to you. When I was in fifth grade I had poison ivy and it was one of the worst things I have ever experienced. It was all over my legs, from my knees down, and it was an itchy, red, blotchy mess. I remember being cooped up in my house, hoping someone would put me out of my misery. My mom covered me in that pink calamine stuff and it just didn't help. I was pink and itchy. Recently, I came down with a twenty-four-hour-bug and I felt like my entire body was shutting down. Literally, like I was on low battery. I couldn't focus on anything. I walked around moaning and groaning, "Oh my gosh, I'm dying. . . ." I know—very dramatic. But at that moment, it felt like I was. But on the positive side (because I always look for the positive in any negative), being sick does make you appreciate being healthy. It reminds me to be grateful when I wake up in the morning and there's no more pounding headache, runny nose, or itchy spots. Yes!

Dogs that shed

I wanna hug 'em, and then I get all this hair up my nose and in my mouth. It sticks to me pretty well; why doesn't it stick to them?

Traffic

LA is infamous for bumper-to-bumper, stop-and-go traffic on the freeway. You literally have to give yourself an extra hour for anywhere you're headed just to be on time. You think you're going somewhere ten minutes away, but not if you're driving into the mess on the 405 or the 101. I read somewhere that one-third of the nation's worst traffic jams are in LA. Can't say I'm surprised; I'm usually sitting smack in

the middle of one, staring out the window.

Pickles

They are the evil cousins of cucumbers. No reason for anyone to put one on my burger or on my plate as a garnish. Don't care how you slice 'em, they're nasty.

Bad Wi-Fi

When I need to read a super-important email and it loads, and loads, and loads. . . . I remember one time I had to submit a paper to a teacher on a deadline and I just could not get that thing to send. I wanted to toss my laptop out a window, but then I realized it wasn't to blame. It was that no-good Wi-Fi. Honestly, is there any reason for it? Can't we figure out a way to make the world one big, happy hot spot?

Mean-hearted cats

Cats who have a 'tude or a chip on their shoulder or are rude. You go over and try and be all sweet and cuddly to them and they growl or hiss or swipe at you. Seriously? I blame it on your owner. What did they do that made you *that* grouchy? I mean, I get it: cats have their own distinct personalities just like people. Even though my cat, Emily, isn't like that, she does need things on her own terms and her own turf. You go over to give her some love and she runs away to her spot in the foyer to lie down. She's like, "Okay, *now* you may approach me. . . ."

School hours

School starts way too early. Would it really be *that* difficult to make first period at noon so we can all catch some z's? I don't think the teachers would mind, do you? Is there any rule that says you have to get up at the crack of dawn to learn? My brain is much more willing to compute complex math equations after the morning shows are over on TV. Just sayin'.

And on a more serious note... how people treat the Earth

It makes me so mad. Can we please show some respect? I get totally bent out of shape when I see someone throw trash on the street and leave it there. I'll ask, "Hey, man, why are you doing that?" and I get this lame response: "Well, someone will pick it up. It's their job." You know what? It's *our* job. It's our responsibility to take care of the earth.

Animal cruelty

I'm an animal lover, so I have zero tolerance for people who abuse or neglect animals in any way, shape, or form. We need to have more awareness that things like poaching and hunting endangered species are inexcusable crimes. I wish more people were willing to speak out on this, to be a voice for defenseless animals who have none. So I'm gonna do it, right here, right now: don't do it. And more than that, do get involved in animal protection organizations so that we can all join together and make our voices heard loud and clear. The way I see it, life is life; why is mine more important than an animal's?

People need to focus more on how we treat the Earth. We act as if we have another place to go.

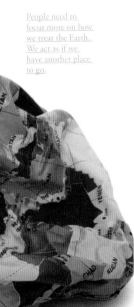

And finally, haters

I don't *hate* haters, because then I'd be a hypocrite. I just don't pay them any mind. I don't want to give them any attention for what they're doing, which is trying their hardest to knock me for being who I am. They have nothing better to do, and I feel bad for them. When I first started out, I didn't know how to handle it—do I respond? Do I not respond? And I had to keep reminding myself it wasn't important. This random dude from Alabama says he doesn't like your Vine—is that gonna stop you from going to LA and making a movie and doing what you want to do? No way! This guy doesn't know me; it's just words on a screen. It's only hate if you let it be hate. Eventually, I learned that it was a waste of my time and energy to try and defend myself. So here's my advice on how to handle the haters in your life: If you look away, if you basically give them no reaction at all, they'll learn that it's pointless; it's not getting to you. You just need to keep moving forward with your life and what makes you happy and not let anyone bring you down. Any negative stuff that haters put out there is really about them and their issues, not you. They only have power if you give it to them. Don't.

Burnie knows he's my right-hand ~~man~~ dog.

#ASKMATT

If junk food was healthy, what would you eat every day?

Chicken nuggets, grilled cheese, french fries, carbs, carbs, carbs, Pop-Tarts, Danimals. I love me some chocolate—I would eat a ton of it every day. I'd have a chocolate salad, seriously.

How many hats do you own, when did you get your first, and why is it the ultimate guy accessory?

I have about one hundred—prob fifty in LA, same amount at home. I got my first really "cool" one for Christmas, when I was young—I liked it because it was not only cool, but it kept my head warm! It's a pretty bold statement when you wear one and also it covers up a bad hair day. Is it the ultimate guy accessory? Don't know about that; I'd put it in the top three. Pair it with sunglasses and cool sneakers, and you are good to go.

What is your all-time fave kids' movie and why?

I was a huge Goofy fan so I saw *A Goofy Movie* a bunch of times. I liked *Shrek*, too. But I think I saw *The Even Stevens Movie* with Shia LaBeouf on the Disney Channel a dozen times or more. It was super lit! I could seriously watch it right now. Where's my remote?

What is your fave scent? Least fave?

I love orange and strawberry scents—fruity, citrusy. Fresh laundry is nice, too. Pizza restaurants. Sheds—I really like the wood smell, like you've been sawing or sanding something. The forest after the rain smells great. Bonfires! I love the smoky scent, but not sure you'd want to wear that on your neck, ya know? My least fave smell would have to be cigarettes—disgusting. Even a whiff makes me gag. Then comes fish, eggs, the odor when my dog poops. That's right; I said cigarettes smell worse to me than feces. Read into it what you will.

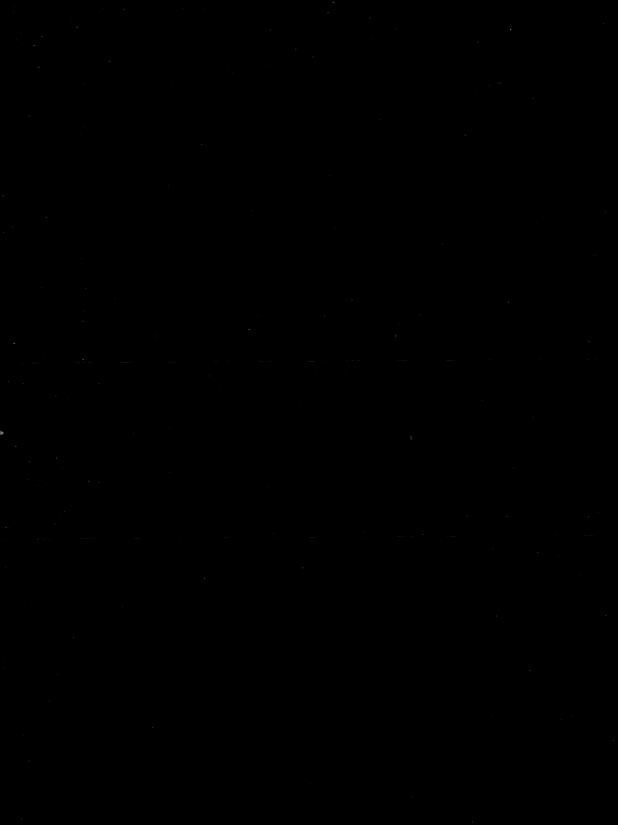

HOW TO BE MY BAE

(04)

BE REAL WITH ME

Here's the thing: when it comes to relationships, I don't believe there needs to be a how-to list or a rule book—at least, I'm not following one. The more you try to make things happen, the more easily stuff falls apart. Things need to happen naturally, and you can't go by someone else's game plan. Every relationship is as unique and individual as the two people involved in it. It should never be about labels ("I'm the boyfriend; you're the girlfriend"). It doesn't need to follow a schedule ("Saturday is movie night"), because that kills all the spontaneity—and life isn't like that, you know? There will be curveballs, and how you face them together is what makes your relationship strong. So if you ask me, I'd say a great relationship is one where you can chill, be yourself, be honest about your feelings, and take your time getting

to know each other. Why does it have to be about pressure or expectations? Why can't it just *be*?

I get asked a lot (usually by reporters) about what I'm looking for in the love department and how I would describe my perfect date. I don't have a shopping list that I keep in my back pocket. I'm not someone who says, "She has to be blond or brunette or a redhead." That's just surface stuff. For me, it's someone's mind or personality that's attractive—that's more powerful than the physical. When I was younger I would get a crush on someone and it would be all-encompassing: "You are the love of my life!" But when you get older, you realize there is more to a person than "Gee, she's cute." There are more things that go into what you find attractive—what's on the inside, not just the outside. I think mature love involves mutual respect. And let me make something clear: dating is not the same thing as being in a relationship. A relationship is something more; it's a deeper connection. I also

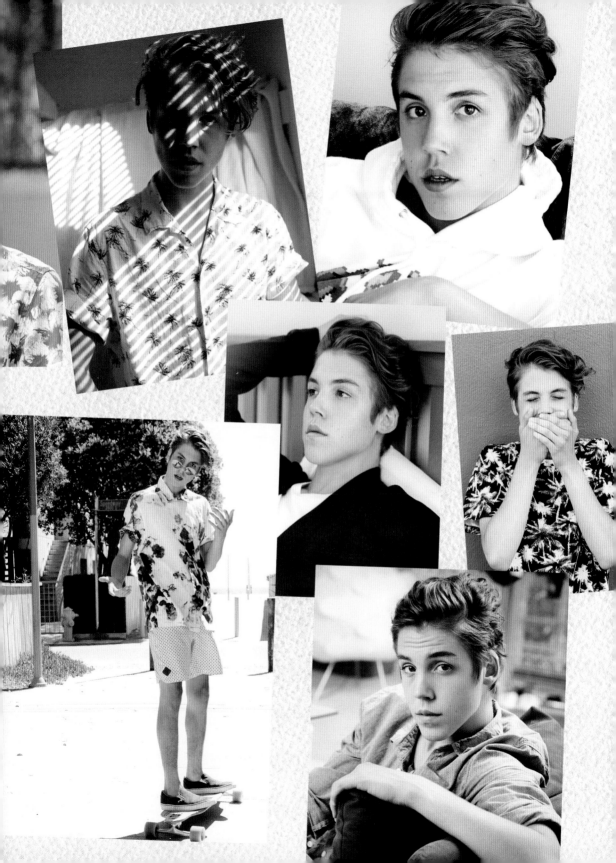

can't tell you "my perfect date." I don't think it should be predictable. Like, snowboarding is a great date. Jumping into a ball pit is a great date. I want to be with someone who is adventurous and down for anything, because that's how I am—I like surprises. I like fun. I like someone who thinks outside the box and would rather play Putt-Putt golf than sit in some stuffy restaurant eating snails.

So, saying what I'm looking for in a relationship, that's a tough one. But here goes nothing:

I WANT TO BE WITH SOMEONE WHO GETS ME AND DOESN'T WANT TO CHANGE ME.

I don't need to pretend to be someone I'm not, and you don't have to put on airs to impress me. I want to know what you think and feel about things, and I want to tell you what's going on in my head, too. There's a mutual respect between us, and an appreciation of what makes us unique—flaws and all.

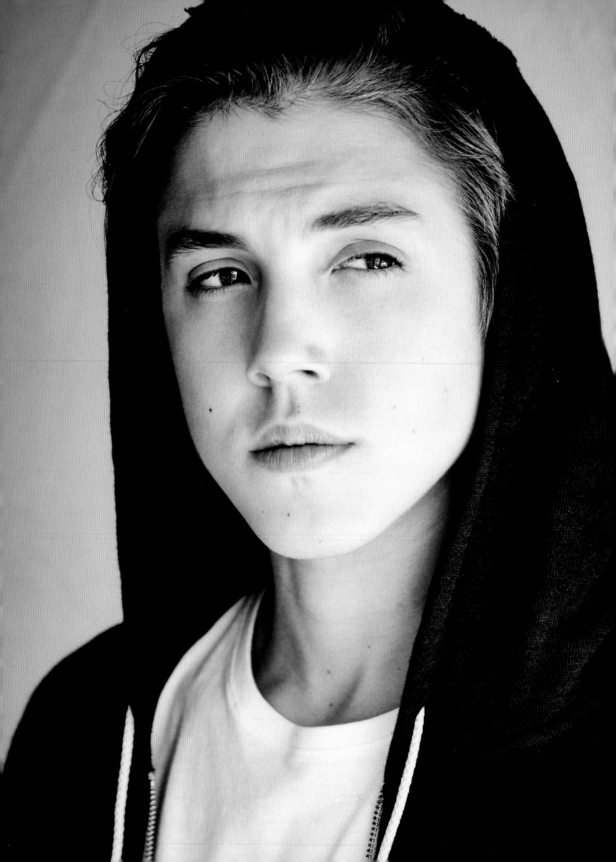

I WANT US TO HANG OUT AND CHILL AND JUST ENJOY EACH OTHER'S COMPANY.

Who says a date has to involve a movie or dinner or going out at all? Can't we just order in a pizza, watch a Disney flick on TV, and snuggle on the couch? I think the best dates are the ones that are not "date-like." That's boring. I want a woman who'll go to the arcade with me and play some old-school Pac-Man and Donkey Kong. If I want to impress a girl, I make it personal. I listen to what she likes, hopes, and dreams, and then one day . . . I make it happen. For example, you tell me, "Every Sunday after church I used to go bowling." A week later, I surprise you with a date to a bowling alley. That right there is special: I'm trying to touch your heart and show you I pay attention when you tell me something. No need to say it twice, I hear ya!

I WANT A GIRL WHO ISN'T AFRAID TO MAKE FUN OF HERSELF AND LOOK GOOFY.

I want someone I can laugh with because, at the end of the day, laugher is my top turn-on. There's no need to ever get so serious. I'm a guy who likes to kid around, tell jokes, prank friends, make a fool out of myself in public if the situation presents itself. The girl who not only laughs at me but laughs *with* me— she's a keeper.

I HAVE TO BE WITH SOMEONE I CAN CONNECT WITH EMOTIONALLY AND INTELLECTUALLY—WE CAN HAVE A SUBSTANTIAL CONVERSATION.

As much as I like to kid around, I'm also a deep thinker. I like to ponder what things mean and talk about the big picture: Why are we here and what can we do to make this world a better

I want someone I can la
end of the day, laug

gh with because, at the

er is my top turn-on.

place? I need someone who listens and cares and has compassion. Bottom line: if all you care about is the latest fashion trend, we are not meant to be.

I WANT A GIRL WHO DOESN'T TRY TOO HARD.

It's okay to let your natural beauty inside shine through. I promise I'll brush my hair and my teeth if you do—but that's all that's required.

I DON'T CARE WHAT EVERYONE ELSE THINKS.

It isn't about your friends or my friends or their friends—they shouldn't have a say in our relationship or judge. It's about *us*. When other people get involved, that's a recipe for disaster. I need a girl who is trustworthy and will talk to *me* openly and honestly—not put it out there for public opinion.

#ASKMATT

Do you see yourself with a wife and kids?
Tomorrow? No. I'm nineteen! But one day, I want a family, for sure. I feel it's the ultimate foundation and your opportunity to shape future generations. Can't you imagine little mini Matthews running around?

Would you ever date a fan?
I don't know. If the universe set one in my path, maybe. Life works in mysterious ways, so you never know.

What is your ultimate turnoff?
Cigarettes. I would never date a girl who smokes. I hate to say never to anything, but that's how I feel.

Are you looking for a girlfriend?
I don't think I'm ever looking for someone. I believe that when we look we become more desperate. I cringe when I see people on Twitter or Instagram who say, "I want to be in a relationship soooo bad." You shouldn't be more in love with the idea of a relationship than with the actual person. For me, if it happens, it happens. The universe will lead me to the right person at the right time. I'll look in her eyes and I'll know. For now, I'm just focusing on my career. A fan asked me, "Do you not have a woman in your life?" I have a lot of women in my life—friends, my sister, my mom, my aunts. And that's fine for now. I just have to have faith that the universe is looking out for me.

So, you're going on your first date— what clothing style do you dig the most?
Whatever you like that makes you feel comfortable! I'm not saying wear your footie PJs or a superhero cape out to dinner (but hey, why not—that shows you have a sense of humor!), but you don't have to worry about what I like. What would *you* like? I wanna get to know the real you, and if you're a jeans-and-tee kinda girl, then you don't have to wear a fancy dress and heels to impress me. Like I said, honesty is the best policy between two people. Let me see who you really are, not who you think I want you to be.

TH

THICK

ROUGH

(05)

&THIN

MEET MY SUPPORTING CAST.

I never had a tough time making friends because, growing up, I felt weirded out if someone was left out of a situation or group. I was always that guy who had friends from every walk of life. I had a core group of friends, sure, but I branched out of that circle because being friends with other people gave me a bigger, better perspective on life. Everyone kind of knew me in my school because I tried my hardest to get to know them. I was like a one-man welcoming committee!

I remember walking down the halls and saying hi to kids,

teachers, coaches, janitors—you name it. How can you not? How can you come and go every day and see people and not attempt to find out anything about them? Where's your curiosity? Where's your humanity? Whenever I did take the time to get to know someone better, we found something we had in common: "What? You like that Xbox game, too?" I've always been someone who likes to reach out and connect—that's one of the reasons social media appealed to me.

I remember back in sixth grade, I got sent to the principal's office because a teacher saw me say to some new kid, "Hey, you wanna be friends?" and thought I was being mean and sarcastic. But I wasn't! I was smiling because I was genuine, not joking. I hate to think of someone feeling lonely or awkward when one kind word can erase all that. I'm a "the more the merrier" kind of guy. You don't have to be best friends with everyone, but I believe in having lots of acquaintances. You can have your tight little inner circle yet still be kind, compassionate, and welcoming of others.

In high school, I had a pretty big inner circle of guys I hung with. But lately, I've been keeping my core smaller. It's because

A family that hangs together stays together.

I've wised up to what friendship really means. When you're as open as I am, people can wiggle in there and use you or abuse you. Then you get into frenemy and fake-friend territory. I only want friends who are there for me 100 percent, who know what's important to me and are more concerned with me keeping up with my work and dreams than keeping up with the next party. My friends have my best interests at heart and they get me. With them I don't have to apologize or make excuses. I used to think that friends were people who you just have a good time and chill with, but now I realize they should bring out the best in you. They should make you want to be a better person when you're around them—which I can truly say my crew does. I count among that group, of course, my family. These are the people I would take a bullet for. I believe you are who you associate with. If you are in a downward spiral, it's because you're attracting the wrong people in your life. Do good things and good people will be drawn to you—period.

My Supporting Cast

Each of my family members has played a huge role in my life, both on a personal level, when I was a kid growing up, and with my career.

My dad still helps with business things here and there, but mostly he oversees the financial aspects of my career, as well as teaching me how to manage my money and giving me many words of wisdom. He also has gone on a lot of trips with me, even traveling with me on the MAGCON Tours. Both he and Ryan went on my tours because I was underage, and it was nice to have family experiencing it all with me. Dad is a good packer—he'd get my suitcase and stuff really organized.

Without him, I dunno what would have happened. I'd probably have no clean underwear!

My mom helps out with a lot, too—she is the photographer and keeper of about a million photos of my entire life, not to mention my finger paintings and report cards. She helps me review potential scripts and has also become quite the travel agent, booking a lot of flights and places to stay for Ryan and me when we travel. Espe-

cially, though, she's my moral compass, the person who reminds me to be true to who I am and never lose sight of what's important.

My brother Ryan is my manager—and we're tight. He graduated from Radford University with a bachelor's degree in business administration in marketing. He helps me creatively with all of my content, is in charge of my business development, and he gets the deals done! But even more than that, he's got my back. He knows what's in my head and the direction I want to be going in. We're a good team—although it's a challenge to live in the same house with your manager! But in the end, even if we disagree on something, we're brothers. I'm really lucky that I've got Ryan to look out for me and guide me through, and I'm so glad that the universe had the stars aligned for us. Just when I was taking off and needed a manager, he was graduating and had the exact expertise I needed. I trust him, and someone I really trust is hard to come by.

I consider my brother Dylan the foundation of the family, the backbone. He speaks the truth and he's a great, unbiased peacemaker. If there's something we don't see eye to eye on

among the six of us, he's the one who referees. He's also an ideas guy and helps a lot with input on videos and business ideas for my career—he is really creative and a great problem solver overall. Dylan has always been there for me without judgment. He really knows how to understand people, and that helps a lot when I need it.

Kristen, my sister, is super creative, so she helps me out on a lot of those aspects of my career. Her main focus is heading up my merchandise line. She was also supporting me on the set of my movie every day, and she's helped me sort my thoughts out for this

book and kept me to a schedule. Here's a fun fact: she's even done my makeup for interviews! When I was in my "I want to be alone" phase, she would hang out with me and my dog, Burnie, a lot. We are really close; she's like a second mom to me. She reminds me to always have fun—which is some-

thing you can forget with all the day-to-day stresses of work. We have similar personalities and she gets my warped sense of humor better than anyone else.

As a whole, my family keeps my feet on the ground, keeps me humble, and helps me focus on what I'm doing and what I need to be doing to achieve my goals and dreams. Living in LA and traveling makes it harder for all of us to be together as much as we were when I was younger, but we still make that a priority. It's never a chore for me to go back home; I want to be there, surrounded by the people who make me stronger, better, more sure of myself. If I ever have a doubt, they're all there to lift me up.

#ASKMATT

What are your favorite random things to do with your family?

Watch movies and TV shows on Netflix. Play games like Super Smash Bros. Go shooting at the shooting range. When we were little we went to the movies, water parks, and amusement parks like King's Dominion. I think we need to revisit that: roller coasters. My siblings and I recently went to an escape room, where you have to work together as a team to get out—that rocked.

What is your most favorite family memory?

Daytona Beach stands out in my mind—go-karting and going to Putt-Putt golf, too. I have so many great family memories, but my head goes to those times in Daytona as fun, fun, fun. We really enjoy being with each other.

What is your dream family vacation?

Hawaii. I think we'd all be down for that. Anywhere tropical where we could chill. We've been to Florida, Colombia, on a couple cruises to the Bahamas, and on several mini-trips

to places in Virginia and nearby states. But a long, extended break somewhere beachy with palm trees would be awesome. Snowboarding would also be great—a family ski trip. The siblings have gone together, but Mom and Dad haven't gone with us. We tried it this past year, but it was a really hot Christmas—record highs—and all the East Coast ski resorts had no snow. So instead, we went south to the Daytona and Miami beaches. Maybe next year. . . .

How would things be different if you didn't have such a strong support team in your family?

It would feel wrong. I have to remind myself how lucky I am. I feel like every single person in my family has been behind me the whole time I've been growing

Aunt Nancy and Aunt Janie have always been there for me. I love y'all! Wesley has my back, too.

my career. They have my best interests in mind 24/7—and I don't know if I could say that about anyone else.

What is one word you would use to describe your family?

Probably "intense." We tend to do things in big ways, maybe because there are six of us and small is not an option? We love intensely, too. We are a passionate family—but in good ways. Or maybe I'd say "one of a kind." But that's four words, not one. Then again, who's counting?

What are your fave things to eat with your family?

Crabs! My dad and mom aren't into it, but the rest of us like to pick those little critters apart. And every now and then, we order pizza. My dad makes an amazing spaghetti that we all chow down on—really garlicky with chicken in it, and my mom's French onion soup is so good, too. I always get excited when she says she's gonna make it—same with my dad's spaghetti!

My friends . . .

- **are genuine.** They don't have ulterior motives for wanting to be my friend. They don't mooch off me or try and call in constant favors. I, however, might mooch off them (just kidding!).
- **are loyal.** They will back me up and stand by me, even when things get complicated.
- **never just tell me what they think I want to hear.** They're genuine and authentic.
- **respect me for who I am** and don't try to change me. And that respect is mutual.
- **tell it to me straight.** I can count on my posse for honest feedback. If something sucks, they don't sugarcoat it. And that's a good thing: sometimes you're too close to something to really see it for what it is. Friends tell you. If I hear, "Matthew, you haven't showered in a week, dude. It's time," I will definitely take it under consideration.
- **are not judgmental.** They don't put me down. Any criticism is constructive and comes from a good place of care and concern. If I have spinach stuck in my teeth or something hanging out of my nose, they will definitely point it out (and hopefully not post it on Instagram).
- **teach me things about myself and life.** Mental stimulation is key; my friends have to make me think. I'm not saying we have to watch *Jeopardy* every night or start a book club, but a little intelligent conversation is appreciated.

Hanging with my class after middle school graduation

When I was younger, my friends and I were always running around each other's backyards. We lived in this cul-de-sac, so the neighborhood kids all hung together, and we kept each other busy. And someone's mom could always keep an eye on us. In high school, we'd go to Panera or Chipotle after school; we'd go mudding or toss a football.

Today, my friends and I hang out in different places—our houses, the beach, the desert, the forest (okay, I guess we're still running around outdoors!). We have this spot in Malibu, a nook on the beach that's kind of a pain in the butt to get to because you have to park really far away and then you have to hike and climb some rocks. It's an adventure. We bring supplies—wood, all the s'mores necessities, guitars and speakers—and we hang there all night. That, to me, is a great time, relaxing under the stars, listening to waves crash on the sand, roasting marshmallows.

I guess things change but they don't change: a guy needs his gang to chill with.

Thumbs-up to this class trip with my friends from fifth grade

I caught my best friend talking to my ex. I feel like she's stabbed me in the back! How could she?

In my opinion, no person should lay claim to any other person. So you dated him, you broke up, and now your friend looks like she might be into him. Um, so what? I only see an issue if your ex was a jerk and you don't want her to get mixed up with him. Otherwise, I don't think you can interfere or get mad at her for feeling the way she does. I say let it be. It's not her fault things didn't work out between you. I get it—it may feel weird or awkward at first because you've got this history with the guy. But people grow up and move on. Maybe this is

#**ASK**MATT

the kick in the butt you needed to get past it.

I feel like nobody gets me and wants to be my friend. How can I make people like me more—and will you be my friend?

Okay, you can't *make* people like you. You can't tie them to a chair and say, "Hey, you, be my friend!" It doesn't work that way. But you *can* make an effort to connect. You *can* put yourself out there. I think sometimes people get stuck in this place of "woe is me" and they build a wall around themselves, not letting others in. If you put the vibe out there—"I'm a good person; I'm worthy!"—I promise you that people will be drawn to you like a magnet. Ya gotta believe it first, and then everyone else will. If you have negative feelings about yourself, that's what you're projecting. And you wonder why no one is eager to hang with you? Also, know that if no one gets you at this moment in time that's not necessarily a bad thing. It means you are mentally and emotionally more in tune with yourself and what you want. If people don't understand you, then they are just not caught up to where you are yet. It will happen; they'll eventually mature. But in the meantime, yes, of course, I will be your friend. And I promise you, I won't be the only one lining up.

Is it better to have lots of friends or one best friend?

One best friend over all. Quality over quantity. If you spend all your time trying to have tons and tons of friends, you're not going to develop quality relationships with anyone. I say, pick a few good people to focus on. I mean, I get it—everyone wants more Facebook "friends," more followers, and people liking them on social media, so it seems like having a lot of peeps in your corner is the way you should always go. But I say one great relationship with someone, something deep and meaningful, is worth a lot more than a huge circle that's shallow.

On My Own

When I was seventeen and I was in LA, I spent a lot of time going out at night with friends. LA kinda comes alive at night, and it was exciting and fun to be here. But when I turned eighteen, I decided it was time to focus and buckle down. The party scene just didn't appeal to me; I didn't feel like being in a crowd. I wanted to shut out the noise, be holed up at home. If it wasn't for work or business, I preferred to stay in. My friends were like, "Hey, dude, are you being a hermit or what?" But it wasn't that at all—I was getting to know myself better.

During this time, Burnie was my best friend. He always kept me company; he made sure I was never completely alone. But I have to admit . . . I kind of liked being at home at night. Being able to be by myself, conquering the aloneness, is a very important part of life and growing up. To be honest, I like the solitude; I appreciate my time with me, me, and only me. One of my friends recently tweeted, "I don't hate you . . . I just love being alone." And that's how I feel. It's not that I don't want to hang out with my crew, it's just I love the time to listen to my own thoughts. I used to see someone sitting in a movie all alone and assume they were lonely or friendless. Now I envy them. They're confident and comfortable; they know it's cool to fly solo. It took me a while to embrace that lesson, but now I got it down. Before you can be a good friend to anyone, you need to be a friend to yourself. You need to be independent and self-reliant and able to stand on your own two feet (or in Burnie's case, his own four paws). Being alone doesn't have to be scary or pathetic. It can be empowering, enlightening, and positive. So now you know where to probably find me on a Saturday night. . . .

So now you know where to probably find me on a Saturday night. . . .

FIVE THINGS I HAD TO LEARN WHEN I GREW UP

01. **How to do laundry**

02. **How to run a dishwasher**

03. **How to really take care of myself and my own place without my parents' supervision**

04. **How to get around from place to place without my mom or dad driving me**

05. **How to deal with being homesick and lonely sometimes**

IN MY OWN WORDS

When I tweet (and I tweet *a lot*) it's not just some random thing. Truly, I think about everything I say before I put it out there in the Twitterverse. I understand the power of words, and I consider that this is my chance to reach out and bond with my generation. Occasionally I might just say, "Hey, what's good?" because I'm curious and wanna connect. Or I might post a fun little thing to make you smile ("Monkeys are so amazing, oh my gosh") or give someone a shout-out ("Love ya, Momma!"). But usually, I'm mulling over, "So what do I want to communicate? What do I want people to think about as they go through their daily lives?" The goal is something uplifting or inspiring, something that makes you think about not just yourself, but the rest of the world

and your role in it. That's the thing: we all have the power to make a change, to do good, to grow, to learn, to be better, to be ourselves. Or we can sit on our butts and let life go by without making an impact. I don't know about you, but that last option is not an option for me. I've been given this platform, this ability to be heard, so I want my words to have a purpose. I think of it like throwing a pebble in a pond—watch the ripple effect. My favorite quotes or lyrics do that for me; they grab me, put things into perspective, and remind me of what's really important. If a day is crappy, then I have my mottoes to turn to for a reality check. Here are a few of my favorites that I live by:

"Keep it simple."

Don't overanalyze, overdo, overstress. Remember there is a beauty to simplicity, to getting down to the basics, to clearing your mind and your life of clutter. Sometimes it's better to just get out of your head, to let go of the stuff holding you back, and focus on the essentials.

"Learn something new each day."

Do something that challenges you mentally, physically, spiritually. Give yourself the opportunity to grow and expand your horizons. There's a lot out there if you're willing to look for it. Growing each day is what life is about. Standing still is not only boring, it makes your feet hurt. . . .

"Let people be."

This is about tolerance, acceptance, compassion. Everyone has a right to their own life and their own opinions. Do your own thing and embrace what makes you special and unique. Copying me or someone else is not giving yourself enough credit. Also, don't judge others. That's not your job. Be chill with everyone; be respectful. Treat people the way you want to be treated. Remember that we all have one thing in common: we're human beings on this planet.

"Bite your tongue."

There are a lot of times you want to say something that is fueled by the wrong emotions: jealousy, anger, frustration, fear. Hit the pause button before you let it rip. Words can help, but they can also hurt; they are a powerful weapon, in many ways more powerful than a gun. So before you speak, consider, are you

shooting at the right person and the right target? I remember when I was young, I would say "I hate you!" to people, and I didn't mean it. I was reacting out of anger, and now I look back and see how wrong that was. Before anything comes out of your mouth, consider the consequences and the motivation. Consider how people might read and respond. I recently tweeted, "I need peeeeeaaacceeeeeee," and I got a ton of comments from people who said, "I thought this said I need to pee!" So clearly, the good intention was there (I want peace for all), but maybe that was one I should have clarified or kept to myself?

They Said It

There are a lot of people I admire for their words—in general, people whose main focus in life is to teach and bring enlightenment, to lift people up, unite them, empower them. They're all on a certain wavelength. I'd love to be a member of this club.

Tom Shadyac

"I think true success is intrinsic . . . It's love. It's kindness. It's community."

"I hope people start to look at their lives as the most powerful, creative act they will ever offer this world."

Dalai Lama

"Happiness is not something that comes ready-made. It comes from your own actions."

"Be kind whenever possible. It is always possible."

Eric Thomas

"You will not stop. You will not quit. You will keep going."

Buddha

"Give, even if you only have a little."

"Hatred is never appeased by hatred in this world. By non-hatred alone is hatred appeased. This is a law eternal."

Morgan Freeman

"People need to start to think about the messages that they send in the movies."

"If you lay down, people will step over you. But if you keep scrambling, if you keep going, someone will always, always give you a hand."

Matthew Espinosa
@TheMattEspinosa

Jus cuz u got the best ride don't mean u the best guy

Matthew Espinosa
@TheMattEspinosa

Don't ever let people know what you're doing... just let them see.

Matthew Espinosa
@TheMattEspinosa

Take me to a secret place

Matthew Espinosa
@TheMattEspinosa

Smile. Even when it's hard to

Matthew Espinosa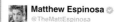
@TheMattEspinosa

I wake up too early sometimes. Oh well at least the early bird gets the worm

Matthew Espinosa
@TheMattEspinosa

Just because you can't understand something, doesn't mean it's wrong.

Matthew Espinosa
@TheMattEspinosa

Follow your bliss and the universe will open doors where there were only walls!

Matthew Espinosa
@TheMattEspinosa

U got the key to some great vibes

Sweet

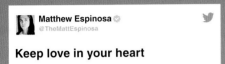

Matthew Espinosa
@TheMattEspinosa

I'm confused... cereal is good tho

Matthew Espinosa
@TheMattEspinosa

I saw a video of a hippo eating a watermelon and it was riveting as heck to say the least

Matthew Espinosa
@TheMattEspinosa

Keep love in your heart

Matthew Espinosa
@TheMattEspinosa

I GOTCHU

Matthew Espinosa
@TheMattEspinosa

be YOU. I know its hard when u got all these people in the media telling you who you should be. the real ones ALWAYS rise. only time tells

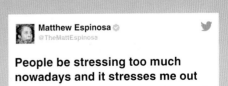

Matthew Espinosa
@TheMattEspinosa

Space doesn't look so intimidating in the daytime

Matthew Espinosa
@TheMattEspinosa

We all have a mission in this life to create something amazing

Matthew Espinosa
@TheMattEspinosa

Driving with square wheels would be difficult

Matthew Espinosa
@TheMattEspinosa

People be stressing too much nowadays and it stresses me out

Tweets

#**ASK**MATT

If you could have a conversation with any person, living or dead, who would you choose?

A real, deep, meaningful, uninterrupted heart-to-heart? I think I would choose Martin Luther King Jr., Mother Teresa, or Pope John Paul II. Then again, I'd like to hear what Michael Jackson or Kid Cudi would have to say, too. There is so much we can learn from listening to each other, don't you think? I mean, I remember being in school when I was younger and kind of zoning out when my teacher lectured us. But now, I think I would have better listening skills. I would wanna soak it all in like a sponge if I had any of the above sharing their words of wisdom with me. No dozing off.

My friend pissed me off and I called her some pretty awful names. I feel like I can't ever take it back and we will never be able to get past this. What should I do?

Well, words got you into this, so let them get you out. Tell her how you feel, that you know you reacted too harshly or quickly without really thinking it through, and if you had it to do all over again, you would choose your words more carefully. If she's a real friend, she'll hear you loud and clear—as clear as she did when you mouthed off. Next time, think first, words second.

If you met the president of the United States, what would you ask him?

If it was Obama, I hear he's into sports. So maybe I'd ask him to play some one-on-one basketball. I'd definitely keep it chill, maybe even challenge him to some Xbox. Can you imagine going against Obama in a game of Call of Duty: Black Ops? How great would that be? What I wouldn't do is ask him about his policy on stuff or tell him how to run the country. Too predictable. He probably gets that all the time. I wanna stand out.

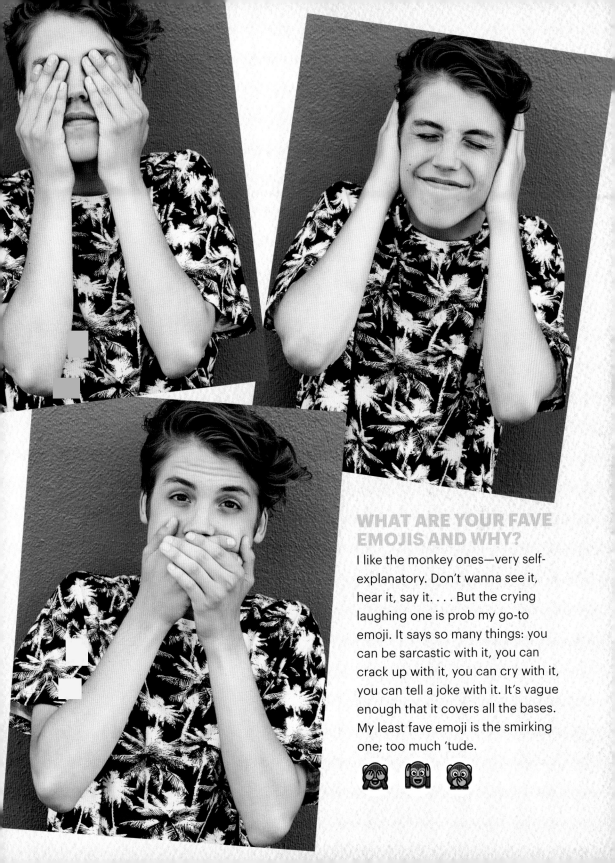

WHAT ARE YOUR FAVE EMOJIS AND WHY?

I like the monkey ones—very self-explanatory. Don't wanna see it, hear it, say it. . . . But the crying laughing one is prob my go-to emoji. It says so many things: you can be sarcastic with it, you can crack up with it, you can cry with it, you can tell a joke with it. It's vague enough that it covers all the bases. My least fave emoji is the smirking one; too much 'tude.

🙈 🙉 🙊

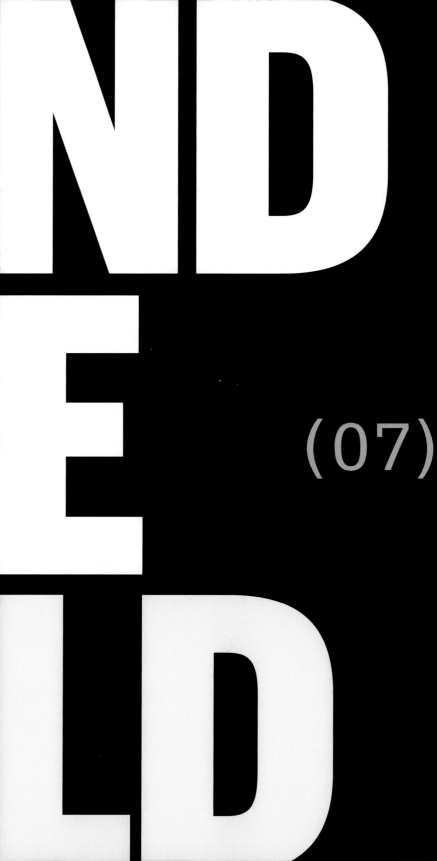

GOING PLACES

The flight to Dubai took sixteen hours—by far the farthest place I have ever traveled. I went there in April 2016 to see friends, meet fans, do some networking, and attend the Social Media Summit. I went with Ryan and some business partners. I was only there for four days, but I felt like every minute was an adventure. I was constantly running into fans and, toward the end of the trip, I had a big meet and greet. I went on a helicopter ride, went to the beach, rode dune buggies and ATVs in the desert, went to a seven-star hotel (who knew they could have that many stars—I thought five was the max!), and to the UN World Food Programme. That was one of the most memorable stops on our trip because I learned so much. The

WFP is one of the largest humanitarian agencies in the world, providing food assistance to more than eighty million people in seventy-five countries. These are the first responders on the scene when tragedies happen, providing food and clean water. The WFP's goal is "zero hunger" on this planet. The people who work at the WFP change lives every day.

I guess I was most surprised by the culture shock I experienced in Dubai—what their way of life is versus how people live in the United States. People look at their phones a lot less; they're not as absorbed in their technology as they are in LA. They're a little more in touch with their lives and living in the moment, which I found refreshing. I was jet-lagged from the flight—I'm not gonna lie—but there was so much to do and see, I powered through it. I love to travel; I don't think you should ever stay in one place. To see how other people live allows you to get a better perspective; you experience things you've never known before, and it makes you  appreciate what you have and also see the many possibilities. Even though I love staying at home, I also love traveling to different places and will make sure to do a lot of traveling in my lifetime. I need to get out and explore. I feel like when I come back from seeing a new place, my head is exploding with ideas.

Dubai is a very new city. Twenty years ago, it was just

flat desert. Now it's all these mile-high skyscrapers with more going up every day. My expectations going there were "it's all big; it's all over-the-top and kind of futuristic." But in reality, it was very sandy, too. Yeah, it's big and bright and shiny—kind of Vegas on steroids. But it's also filled with very warm, very genuine people. I have to say, I was really touched by the fans and the outpouring of support there. I wish I'd had more time to really get to experience it all; it was intense, and the only downtime I had was when I went to my hotel to sleep. I'd like to say it was the coolest place I've ever been, but it's pretty early to say that in my lifetime. Definitely top five, and I know I'll be going back.

I brought home a bunch of souvenirs for my family. Myself, I'm not much of a souvenir guy. I'd rather snap pics and videos and experience as much as I can. The memories are my souvenirs.

MY TRAVEL
PHOTO ALBUM

ENGLAND

I went to England once while on tour. I remember the streets being pretty wild and a little scary. But I really loved the weather there and the historic vibe. I look forward to going back one day.

COLOMBIA

My dad is from Cartagena, Colombia. My family and I visited there for the very first time in the summer of 2010. I actually had my thirteenth birthday there, and my aunts even planned a birthday party for me! While we were there, we also went to the wedding of one of my cousins. I met so many more family members on my dad's side, and we had so much fun. My dad also showed us all around Cartagena, including El Centro, the historic section of Cartagena, and also the island of Manga, where he lived when he was a teenager.

COLOMBIA

We took a boat ride to a private island. On the way to the island, we actually stopped in the middle of the water and met up with a fisherman in a boat who had live lobsters for us to choose from, and we cooked them on the island. That was a really cool experience I never thought I'd have. Overall, it was an amazing trip that I learned a lot from and I will never forget. I love Colombia because it is part of who I am, and I can't wait to go back!

DUBAI

I rode a camel for the first time. It was a lot of fun—I named the camels Chester and Sylvester. I didn't really intend for the names to rhyme, but hey, it works. The ride was a little bumpy, but I got used to it.

DUBAI

The helicopter took us around Dubai. The one thing that really stood out was the Burj Khalifa, the tallest building in the world—it's 160 stories. I had my meet and greet inside there, which was crazy. I got to go the top of the tower and look down. The view is insane. Everyone below looks like ants.

DOMINICAN REPUBLIC

I was only in the Dominican Republic for one day. But one thing that really stood out to me was the humidity! Also, it was culture shock seeing how many people live so differently than we do. For instance, they rode a lot on motorcycles and ATVs rather than in cars. I'd like to go back and visit again when I have more time.

CANADA

I also went to Canada while on a tour. It wasn't as cold as I had expected. The people there were really nice. I was only there for a short time, but I had a blast!

HING

LITERALLY AN OPEN BOOK

I have said I will always be open and honest with my fans—
my life is an open book (did ya get that pun?). So here, without
further ado, are your craziest, weirdest, most perplexing
questions answered to the best of my abilities.

I wonder who
took the first
selfie. . . .

I'm confused: What should I call you? Matthew, Matt, Matty?

I would say Matthew. I feel like Matthew is a whole different name than Matt. I gotta stand up for it. It means "gift of God," so that's pretty cool. You could call me Matty, I guess, for fun. If I'm ever wearing a suit, I'll call myself Classy Matty. But just so ya know, my mom calls me Matthew. And what Mom says goes.

Would you ever shave your head?

I waxed my legs once on a dare, does that count? I did actually shave my head when I was in sixth grade. I didn't go totally bald, but it was a pretty close buzz. I wouldn't do it again—at least not anytime soon. I don't see the need. My hair keeps my head warm and toasty.

What scares you more, snakes or spiders?

Oh, snap! I get chills just thinking about it. I think I would have to go with snakes, unless the spiders were huge tarantulas. But neither one makes me particularly happy.

If you could go back to a time in your life again, what year would you pick?

Maybe the summer before I was a freshman in high school—one of the best summers of my life. That was the last summer I had before I started getting big, and it was one of my last free-feeling summers; no work, no pressure; just chilling with family and friends. My summers have been very different since then. Or maybe sophomore-year football season, the last three games. We had the best record in school history. I was with such a great group of kids. Every single day after school we were on the field, and we played and we played and we played. The team was my family. When I get random memory flashbacks, that's what comes to me and puts a smile on my face. I'll never forget it; I could almost tell you every single play. I get goose bumps thinking about it. It's ingrained in my brain.

Would you ever get a tattoo or piercing?

Personally, I don't think I would get a tattoo. If I did, it would be very small and it would mean something really special to me, something I could take to the grave. I think people sometimes get tattoos for the wrong reason—it's not just an accessory you can put on. It's there forever, and ever, and ever. Piercings? Well, I did have my ears pierced for a bit. . . .

What is your greatest strength?

I guess I would say I'm a take-charge kind of guy. I'm good at being a leader; I don't worry about the problem, I shift right into solution mode. I'm also pretty confident in any move I make.

What is your greatest weakness?

I'm not great at trusting people. It makes me hesitant about putting myself out there and opening up to new people, because I'm always a little suspicious of their motives. It's why I like lying low and flying under the radar sometimes. I'm really choosy about the people I surround myself with—which I guess could be a strength as well as a weakness.

If I scanned through your internet browsing history on your phone, what would I find?

Xbox 360 games, some throwback stuff—a Pokémon hoodie I just bought on Amazon. Manhattan Bagel (I was searching them to see if I could find them in LA). I looked up a light shop for some cool lights. I probably have fifty random tabs open on my phone at any time.

What do you want your tombstone to say?

Okay, a bit of a creepy question, but 'cause you asked, I'll go for it: "Matthew Espinosa: Legend." Heroes are remembered but legends never die—isn't that what they say? Or how about, "Matthew Espinosa: The Man Who Changed the World." Yeah, I'd be happy in the ever after with that on my stone—but only if I earn it.

What is one of your fave quotes?

"Don't cry because it's over, smile because it happened." My philosophy.

Do you exercise?

Not regularly, not as often as I probably should, and I've been trying to do it more recently. When I was playing football and sports, I worked out every day. Nowadays I go through spurts, but when I travel it's tough. When I do work out, I'll do weight lifting, arms and back one day; maybe legs the next. I don't want to be bulky, just lean. I might do a mile or two on the treadmill, too. Some people hate to sweat, but I'm okay with it. Although my hair's pretty long, so it's kind of annoying. And it was really humid the other day. Think I'm looking for excuses? Nah . . .

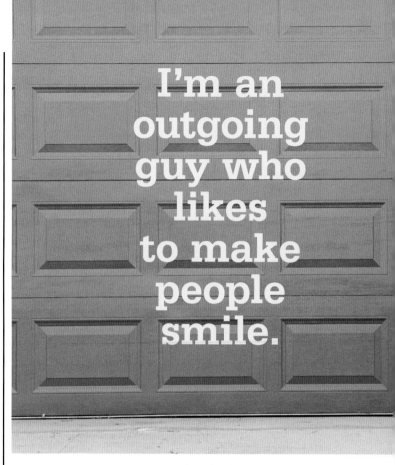

I'm an outgoing guy who likes to make people smile.

Would you rather be ugly or ignorant—if you couldn't change either of these things?

If I couldn't change it, then I think I'd rather be ugly, because I believe beauty is in the eye of the beholder and there is someone out there for everyone, someone who will find me attractive. I'd rather know more than look good. I'd go for the beautiful mind. I think it's worse not to have knowledge and not be able to change that.

What is in your fridge?

Strawberries. Lots of strawberries. Lots of cheese. Eggs, milk, OJ. A couple of Smartwaters. Ranch dressing, some salad, Cool Whip (to

go on the strawberries if I'm feeling a little crazy). Hot Pockets—but those are kind of more my bro Ryan. Danimals and Go-Gurts. I'm pretty basic; keep it simple. Some people have a whole bunch of ingredients to make a cool omelet. I'm an egg-and-cheese kinda guy.

What would I find in your car trunk? Under your bed?

I have a car but I don't drive it. I have to say, I'm pretty neat, so you won't find much. Maybe in my trunk, some stuff from when I went snowboarding recently. Some empty water bottles. Under my bed? A few dust bunnies, but that's it.

What is the meanest thing anyone has ever said or done to you?

One time this kid punched me in the face in sixth grade, but I kind of asked for it. I took things too far; we were playing basketball, and you know how guys get into it. It didn't knock me off my feet. I was standing there in shock, and right after, before I could even hit him back or yell, he ran behind the biggest kid in school and hid. It wasn't his best idea, but I gotta give

him props for making such a bold move. We're actually friends now, which is funny—two or three weeks later we made up. It all worked out. Random people on social media have been pretty mean, but I don't let them get to me.

Would you rather burn the roof of your mouth on a slice of pizza or have a paper cut?

The paper cut is worse—because that lasts and lasts and you gotta look at it. When you burn your mouth, it hurts, but then it's over. And you at least had the joy of getting to eat the slice, so the pain is worth it.

Finish this poem: "Roses are red, violets are blue . . ."

Cereal is good for me, what about you?

I would say call me Matthew. I feel like Matthew is a whole different name than Matt.

How would you describe yourself to someone who has never met you?

An outgoing guy who likes to make people smile. It's hard to explain yourself to anyone else! Funny. Friendly. Thoughtful.

Do you talk to yourself?

In my head, I have a whole dialogue. I ask myself stuff, then I answer. It's how I problem solve.

If your dog, Burnie, could talk, what would he say?

"I'm so sick of hearing all your silly human problems. Chill out." I don't really think about what he would say, more how he would say it. I always try and imagine his voice. Maybe he'd have a fancy British accent, something royal: "I'm Burnie the Fifth." That would be hilarious.

Do you sing in the shower?

When I'm in the mood I might rap a couple bars.

If you couldn't be Matthew Espinosa, who would you be?

Morgan Freeman for sure. Or I would prob want to be someone who deals with animals, someone at a wildlife sanctuary who has access to really exotic creatures. Maybe a talented musician who could play piano really well? But overall, I'm really happy with who I am.

What do you put on a pizza?

Just cheese.

In your coffee?

Hate coffee. Skip the coffee, bring me the milk.

On your burger?

I've been doing the same thing my entire life: lettuce, tomato, onion, cheese, and mayo. Five ingredients to a good vibe.

On your waffle?

Strawberries only. No whipped cream, sprinkles, or ice cream on a Belgian. That's moving into dessert territory, you know? Keep it on a breakfast level.

If you had a talk show, what would it be called and who would you ask to be on it?

I'd call it *Chatty with Matty*. And I would talk to a lot of people who are focused on changing the world and keeping good energy going around. I'd also have actors and comedians to keep it lighthearted; my friends and family; my dog, Burnie; the midget dude from the movie *Elf*; Harry Potter; Craig Feldspar from *Malcom in the Middle*.

What's the one question you wish someone would ask you but no one never has?

That one!

IF I
COULD
TALK
ANIMAL

TO

S

(09)

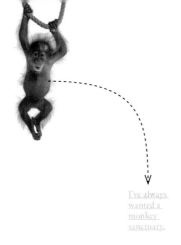

I've always wanted a monkey sanctuary.

I LOVE ALL OF 'EM

I love animals—and I think we as humans have a lot we can learn from them. Elephants, polar bears, and dolphins are all at the top of my list. I love monkeys for their cute playfulness, and I think lions are cool because they're the kings of the jungle. Penguins are pretty dope—they come wearing a tux; turtles are fun, but I don't quite understand how the whole shell thing works; sloths are just sloths and they own it. I'm fascinated by otters—did you know they hold hands when they sleep so they don't drift away when they're floating in the water? Camels have two humps and they spit. Come on, how cool would it be to just spit all day?

Siberian tigers are pretty exotic. Hippos are awesome; I'd love to raise a baby hippo, but I hear they get easily agitated and can grow up to be pretty dangerous. I did a report on hippos once for school and I learned that if a hippo is chasing you, you should run in zigzags. It confuses them.

I love dogs in general. If I could have any one type it would be a pit bull–lab mix. Pit bulls are really sweet, one of the nicest dogs; I know they have a bad rap, but I've never met one that wasn't a big ol' mush. The meanest dogs I've met are usually the little ones. They've got some kind of complex about being small. They will bite your toes off.

Of course, Burnie is my fave animal. We've taught him a few tricks: sit, shake paws, give a high-five. He can balance a treat on his nose. I'll say "wait" and he will. Then he'll flip it in the air when I tell him it's okay and catch it in his mouth. Sometimes we play "Burnie in the middle" and play ball with him. The other day Burnie was looking for something, and I said, "Are you looking for your dinosaur? Go check upstairs." And he did and brought it back down. Burnie understands English. And he doesn't age. He's been the same size, the same energy level, for like four years now. He has his own social media account: he has 230 thousand followers on Instagram (@simplyburnie). Burnie is a celeb. I am in awe of his star power.

My favorite cats are black ones. I'm pretty biased, because my cat, Emily, is black. Okay, here is a fun fact: my initials are MLE, for Matthew Lee Espinosa. And our cat's name is Emily. Get it— MLE sounds like Emily? Okay, these are the things that amuse me. Emily Espinosa is the best. I actually used her in a lot of my Vines. She was a good sport about it! I like the short-haired cats that are playful and act like dogs. I like colorful ones, too—like calicos. I'm really bad with cat breed names. The hairless ones creep me out a little, I have to be honest.

Growing up, my brother Dylan had a hamster named DAFE (those are Dylan's initials) and lost him. He got out of his cage once and we found him, then he did it again the next night. He was like a James Bond hamster; he was sly. He escaped that second time and we never found him. I hope he was a mighty hamster and made it. I hope he found himself a wife and settled down and established his hamster dynasty. I hope he went out into the woods and is a happy great-great-grandfather hamster today.

We also had Lorenzo. He was a snapping turtle that our dad found in our driveway when he was the size of a silver dollar. My dad let us keep him. We put him in a tank and he grew, so we had to keep putting him in bigger tanks. Eventually, he got really big and if you put your finger in the tank, he'd try to bite it off. We had him for two or three years in a small tank and he stayed the same size and was totally manageable and cute. But when we put him in the bigger tank, he ballooned up overnight. It was like he knew that he had more room, so he could stretch his legs. Lorenzo was a little cranky, but I guess snapping turtles are supposed to snap. When he got bigger, he kind of looked like a dinosaur. He was like our family guard turtle. Come too close and he'll chew you up! He actually escaped one time and we eventually found him two weeks later behind our dishwasher! There was a small opening next to it that he somehow managed to crawl through. That's when my dad decided to take him to a fenced-in pond at a park near us that is specifically for turtles. I'm sure he's much happier there.

Ever since Snappy ran away, I've wanted another turtle.

We also had a bunch of hermit crabs we brought home from a trip to Florida. None of us knew how to take care of them, so they croaked literally a day or two after we got them home. The long fourteen-hour drive in our big van probably did them in. We still

As a generation, we have an obligation to protect animals.

have the old cages and shells. We also had a few escapees who managed to get free. They were probably that determined to get away from the Espinosa family: "Let us outta here!" They heard that DAFE peaced out, so this was not the house to be in. We had a bad rap in the small-pet world.

I truly believe that animals are better than people the majority of the time. They work off instinct; they keep it simple. Humans make it complicated. Pets also know how to love with every fiber of their being. If pets are ever mean, that's based on the way they were raised by a human. Most animals aren't malicious; they usually hurt or kill out of fear and defense, or to nourish themselves. They love and protect with all their hearts and souls. They're pure. Their emotions and their motivations are pure.

As a generation, we have an obligation to protect animals. And it starts with the basics: Recycle. Prevent global warming. Protect their habitats, protect the planet, be aware of what's happening on Earth and the places they live. Don't throw your trash on beaches or in the water. There are organizations that work to help. Get involved; donate when you can: the ASPCA, the Humane Society, the International Fund for Animal Welfare, which Leo DiCaprio is involved in. Animals feel. They have emotions just like we do. They feel fear and pain and loneliness. Absolutely, 100 percent. I've seen dogs who look depressed because their owners aren't taking good care of them or paying attention to them. I think that pets are only here to love us and we should then do the same for them. We need to spread the word that we are the keepers of this planet and all its inhabitants.

I think Burnie's jealous that I've got a new furry friend.

ME ON THE BIG SCREEN

(10)

THE BIG SCREEN

I had seen a lot of scripts before I picked *Be Somebody*. I guess what I was looking for in a role was a message I could get behind. In a nutshell, it's about this boy who's finding himself through this girl, an artist who is putting herself out there. She's a high school student from a small town, and she helps him on this whole journey of self-discovery. Jordan is a pop sensation, and he's running away from his tour and the stress he's built up from the life he lives. He's been famous for years, his mom is his powerhouse manager, and he's seen everything, been everywhere, and he just wants to be a regular guy. He's trying to understand what it is to have a real life. I hope my fans take away the message about being

yourself and finding who you are, because it's an important one.

PLAYING JORDAN

There are some things I can definitely relate to in Jordan, but he's not Matthew Espinosa. The whole singing thing—that's not me. And I'm nowhere as famous as he is or as experienced in the whole fame game. But the idea of wanting to figure out who you are and own it, that's universal. That speaks to me. I like that he's a character who wants to be himself, not what people want him to be or expect him to be. I like that he has the courage to take a chance and change his life for the better.

MOVIES VERSUS SOCIAL MEDIA

When you make a movie as an actor, you're taking on someone else's ideas and bringing them to life. In this case, I was stepping into my character's shoes, helping the director, Joshua Caldwell, achieve his vision. In a lot of ways, you're giving up control and trusting someone else to take you where you need to be. On social media, I'm both the actor and the director. I call all the shots. Was it different for me? Yeah. But in a good way. I learned a lot, not just about the process, but about myself as an actor and how a director frames the shot and gives you the tools to dig deep into your character and find his motivation. I want to direct movies eventually. I want to be a director like Quentin Tarantino and other outstanding directors.

ON LOCATION

We filmed for about three weeks in multiple locations around California. The hardest part was the schedule—the twelve-hour days, shooting in the cold. There would be times when I thought I had a break and we'd have to shoot or reshoot: "Oh, okay . . . you need me again?" Not a lot of downtime. The best part was having this first experience—learning and growing as an actor and seeing the final results—and getting to meet all of these professionals who shared their knowledge with me and showed me the ropes.

THE CAST

Sarah Jeffery plays Emily, and she was amazing to work with. Tava Smiley played my mom, and we had this great, long conversation where she told me what she's learned along the way in her career. My other costars were Allison Paige and LaMonica Garrett. Funny story on him: I was on a flight back from Dubai and this movie, *Daddy's Home*, comes on with Will Ferrell and Mark Wahlberg. I'm watching it, and there's LaMonica, the dude we just cast in my movie and worked with! I learned a lot from all the people on the movie, the cast, the crew, the creative team. I saw the way they worked and maneuvered and I mimicked that. I learned it's not so much acting as it is *being*: Who are you as this character, in this moment? I learned how to memorize long paragraphs of lines quicker. I learned how to react more on camera—which is very different from stage acting. I felt like everyone was really giving and sharing and it was fun getting to know one another.

A FUNNY THING HAPPENED ON SET . . .

There were a bunch of snails one night—an empire of them on this patch of grass. It was in between shots and we were all gathered around watching them, mesmerized. Another time Burnie was on set one night, and he was great—a perfect actor; a natural star. To blow off steam, we would have random dance parties in the trailer.

#**ASK**MATT

What is your movie dream role?

Any hero—a guy who saves the day. Dang, who is that kid? No tights, though. No costume. Just a kid hero.

If you had to choose between being a movie star or a world leader, what would you pick?

Wow . . . that is really hard. At the end of the day, I'd say a world leader, because that's my opportunity to make a difference and do something for the greater good. That's what I feel my purpose is on this earth. I want to use acting as a stepping-stone to be a world leader, make movies about things that get people's attention, bring truth to cinema, activism through film. But not in a documentary way, in an entertaining way that raises awareness. So I guess if I could cut right to it, yeah, I'd say world leader.

Who would be your dream costar (female) and why?

Angelina Jolie, Jessica Alba, Sarah Silverman, or Jennifer Aniston. I would want one of them to play my mom in the movie. They would teach me the kung fu way. I've never seen a movie where the mom teaches the son; it's always the dad. So I'm down for that.

Hanging on set
with my costar
Sarah Jeffrey

It felt like summer camp in a lot of ways. My sister, Kristen, was on set with me every day, which was cool, helping out, running lines with me. Couldn't have done it without her!

BEHIND THE SCENES

As executive producer, I was involved in the whole process, even the casting. Postproduction I saw a rough cut and gave feedback—what I thought was missing, what I thought needed to come out. I also had a say on the music. I felt really trusted and respected the whole time. It was a great collaboration.

WHAT'S NEXT?

We premiered it in June 2016, and it went out in select theaters and is available on a bunch of other platforms, like Netflix, iTunes, On Demand, and Amazon. I did a lot of social-media promoting to help get it out there—a countdown on Instagram and Twitter, where I posted a scene from the film to get everyone hyped up. I'm excited. People asked me if I would read my reviews. Maybe. I don't necessarily want the approval of others; I'm confident with what I've done and I don't care what the critics have to say unless it's constructive. If you are writing something to help me learn and grow as an actor, then there's a better chance I'll read it.

I want to do more movies for sure, and I want to choose every role so specifically and so carefully. I'm gonna keep going with that mindset. I want to make my own movies from start to finish. Now that *Be Somebody* is out, I want to shop myself around more and audition more, and I actually have something to show people: "Hey, look! This is what I can do besides my social media stuff." It's a huge step for me and super exciting. I feel like it's a whole new chapter in my life.

WHAT

(11)

IF...

JUST A DREAMER

I have an active imagination, so I like to envision
all kinds of scenarios (some pretty crazy) and what I would
do in that situation.

If I had wings . . .

I would fly to Egypt, swoop over the pyramids and the Sphinx, then to islands like Maui in Hawaii, where there are beautiful blue waters that I could get a bird's-eye view of. I'd fly to Narnia (yeah, I think it's a real place), and I'd fly to Virginia to see my family and friends.

If I had one superpower, it would be . . .

to control time. I'd save the world. I'd go in the future, see the problems, then I'd time-warp back and fix them all before they could occur.

If I was president of the United States . . .

I don't think I would want to be the president. It's too much responsibility; it's not me. The job description doesn't fit my personality. I would want more freedoms as a human being, not to be cooped up in a white house, answering to all these politics.

If I was an astronaut . . .

I would go to Saturn—I think seeing the rings up close would be cool. The whole antigravity thing would be awesome. I would use toothpaste and try to get it on my toothbrush but it would probably just drift on into space. Or I'd eat a burger and fling all the layers—the lettuce, the cheese, the onions, the patty, the bun—like a Frisbie and try and stack 'em up midair. I'd make my own burger-fly game. I think peeing in space would be bizarre; I hope it doesn't float in the air, too. These are the things I think about.

If I was an animal . . .

I would probably be a bird, because they can fly. Or a lion—'cause they're fierce. Or a sloth. Or a koala. Or a monkey named Dayvon or Dmitry. Okay, that's my final answer! I'd still feel humanlike, but I could swing from trees and be adorable.

If I had limitless money . . .

I'd give food to everyone in the world. I'd make sure no one ever went hungry again. I'd do all I could to make sure my family was safe—maybe buy them a bunker in case some scary worldly stuff ever went down. I'd want them to be safe no matter what.

If I was stranded on a desert island . . .

I'd look for food. And shelter. And a really heavy tree. I'd gather up branches. You know, the stuff you see on *Gilligan's Island* or *Survivor*. I'd go into survival mode—all hunter-gatherer or Tarzan. I'd try to get a fire going, maybe catch a fish. Of course, this is assuming I could do all of the above, because if you've ever tried rubbing two sticks together to make a fire, it's pretty impossible. I'd do whatever I could to stay alive. Don't think I'd really wanna be in that situation!

If I was the greatest magician in the world . . .

I'd create this illusion where my head falls off. It would be rolling there on the ground, with the eyes still blinking and my lips still talking. Creepy, yes, but no one would ever forget it. Houdini, move over.

If I could go back in time . . .

I'd probably head back to the seventies or the nineties in Hollywood. There were a lot of cool entertainers then; I'd hang with Will Smith, Jim Carrey, Michael Jackson, Clint Eastwood, and a young Morgan Freeman. We would be tight.

If I was the last dude on Earth . . .

I would go to the beach. I would break into huge mansions and check 'em out. I would go to the supermarket and snag anything I wanted off the shelves. I would have a really good time for about two to three days, then I would get sad and lonely. I think I could stay occupied a lot longer than most people because I genuinely enjoy being alone. I could make the most of it. But in the end, it would stink.

If I was making a movie of my life . . .

I can't even think about my co-stars or what I would title it—I feel like that's thirty or forty years in the future, and I don't have a crystal ball. So I'll say I'll table that one for a few more years to come.

If I was my dog, Burnie . . .

I would sleep, bark, fetch balls. I wouldn't eat dog food. I would hold out until my owner gave me the good stuff, the filet mignon. My day would be short because I'd be playing and sleeping and that would be it. Burnie bliss.

If I was an imaginary creature . . .

I'd be a dragon, hands down. Fire-breathing flying creatures? Does it get any fiercer? I'll go even further: I would be a dragon who has the ability to be invisible. That would be even sicker. My sister, Kristen, says she wants to be a pegasus/unicorn, and that's pretty and magical and all, but no horse with wings is gonna beat my fire-breathing invisibleness. Just sayin'.

If I could be any professional athlete . . .

I would be a pro basketball player. I'd want to be on the Washington Wizards; maybe I'd be Gilbert Arenas. And I'd never miss a shot. Ever.

BE
BODY

(12)

I MEAN IT. GO & BE SOMEBODY.

Yeah, it's the name and message of my movie (imagine that!). But it's also my philosophy. I feel that everyone should try to be somebody in his or her lifetime. As a generation, we are truly unique: the world is at our fingertips thanks to social media and the internet. We have the ability to get the word out through so many more outlets than our parents or their parents did. We have the speed and the power and the avenues to make our voices heard. We can communicate with literally millions of people in a few keystrokes. Posting funny stuff is fine (don't knock it till ya try it). But we also need to be talking about real things, about what is going on in this world, the good and the bad, and what needs to be different.

Think you don't know enough? Knowledge is power, and the internet puts everything within our reach. Educate yourself: Wonder what global warming is? Go on, Google it. Previous generations didn't have that; they would have to go to a library or pick up a newspaper or magazine to learn what was going on in the present or the past. We can access information (provided you have decent Wi-Fi!) in a split second. I think with that ability comes responsibility. What are you going to do with your life that will have an impact? How will you right

wrongs and make the Earth a better place for everyone who lives on it? I know—it's a lot to think about. But we owe it to ourselves and future generations not to just sit back and pass the buck to someone else.

I spend a lot of time pondering, "What's my role and what can I do?" Maybe you've thought about it, too—or maybe I just planted that seed in your mind. Either way, this is your chance, your moment. . . .

01

Start local.

Your town, your city, your community, your church, your school. I always like to think of it as "one hand is for yourself; the other hand is for others." Be proactive. If you see a kid being bullied, stand up for him or her. If you see something that needs fixing, get a group of friends together and set those wheels in motion. It's really pretty simple: keep your eyes open for opportunities to bring about positivity, even in small ways. There is opportunity to make a difference everywhere, every day. And you get really good at finding those opportunities when you look for them.

02

Set a good example.

Be the change you wish to see in the world. Don't just talk the talk; walk the walk. Take care of the Earth. Treat others with respect and kindness: "So in everything, do unto others what you would have them do to you." It's the little things that count. Open a door; say please and thank you; rescue a cat out of a tree. Be polite, be genuine, be responsible. Those are a whole lot of things to "be" but they're the key. If we all did one or two little random acts of kindness a day, the world would be a pretty awesome place.

03 | 04 | 05

Don't judge.

Imagine what it might be like to be in someone else's shoes. Don't make assumptions based on appearance or what others are saying (gossip is never a good source of info). And don't be afraid to go against the popular way of thinking. You're old enough and smart enough to make your own decisions about people and not get caught up in politics. Be open-minded. I was always the welcoming committee in school for the new kids; I would go up to them and introduce myself and find out who they were. Getting to know someone on a personal level is the only way you can make an accurate call. I'm also a big believer in giving people the benefit of the doubt; we're all composed of so many different layers, and you gotta be willing to dig a little deeper.

Dream big.

Not just for yourself, but in a way that we can make this world a better place. We can make a difference; we can be the optimists who see the possibilities and the potential. I am not a fan of those "glass half empty" types who are negative, negative, negative. I'd rather look on the bright side. Let's face it, the world is full of bad news. But what if we chose not to accept that? What if we said, "Yes, there are problems and things that are wrong, but we can turn it around?" I'm a pretty "up" guy, and that's why: where other people might give up because things are too messed up or complicated, I see the possibility for good to conquer all.

Hear people out.

This is a big one. Everyone has an opinion, and while it might not be yours, it's just as valid. I admit it: I'm guilty of sometimes thinking my choice is the only way to go. I'm so sure of it, I don't want to hear someone tell me otherwise, so I kind of tune them out. But then my brothers, Ryan and Dylan, my sister, Kristen, or my mom or dad will say, "Well, what about *this*?" Hmmmm . . . good point. I never would have thought of that. Just by listening, you might find a solution you didn't know existed. You might find the answer you've been searching for. At the same time, you're showing that you have respect and regard for others and you're not a jerk who thinks he or she is right 100 percent of the time. Win-win, don't you think?

Acknowledgments

I want to thank my dad, mom, Kristen, Ryan, and Dylan. Especially to my mom and dad, thank you for your guidance ever since I was born. And to all of you, you guys are my supporting team, and I am so grateful for all you have done and continue to do for me. You helped make this whole book possible, and I couldn't have done it without you!

Shout-out to my writer, Sheryl Berk, and my team at HarperCollins, led by Sara Sargent: Thank you all for your expertise and hard work. Another shout-out to my photographer, Chris Eckert, for making this book so visually pleasing.

To my grandparents and my half sister, Melanie, rest in peace. You'll always be in my heart. I also want to thank the rest of my family, friends, fans (#Espinosas), teachers, coaches, and God for the support, the love, and all the unforgettable memories I've been so blessed to share with you all in this book. Looking forward to many more to come! Much love!

Ever since he was a kid, Matthew Espinosa was looking for a spotlight to perform in and to show everyone who he was. He cultivated a deep love for acting, creating, and humor, and finally discovered Vine as a way to share himself with the world. One billion loops and fifty million YouTube views later, Matthew has become a global phenomenon. After wrapping a hugely successful national headlining tour in 2015, Matthew continued his meteoric rise to fame by starring in *Be Somebody*, his first feature-length film, distributed by Paramount Pictures in 2016.

And this is only the beginning. You can visit Matthew online at www.thematthewespinosa.com.